Made in the USA
Las Vegas, NV
10 March 2021

19368213R00056